C000025586

the

MODERN
MAMIL

A CYCLIST'S A-Z

kinkajou

The Modern MAMIL, A Cyclist's A-Z

Published by Kinkajou

You can find The Modern MAMIL on www.facebook.com/modernmamil

Reproduced courtesy of Yellow House Art Licensing.
www.yellowhouseartlicensing.com

A catalogue record for this book is available from the British Library.

Kinkajou is an imprint of Frances Lincoln Limited
74–77 White Lion Street
London N1 9PF
www.kinkajou.com

ISBN: 978-0-7112-3759-9

Printed in China

the MODERN MAMIL

A CYCLIST'S A-Z

You've hit 40 (or you'll be there soon).

The mirror suggests you need to get into shape. Football is a long forgotten dream and the gym membership has so far cost you £300 per visit. A few friends suggest joining them for a bike ride . . .

. . . you're addicted.

A steady swipe of plastic at your LBS* later and you've become the proud owner of the stiffest carbon on two wheels and a skin-tight outfit for every season.

Weekends are spent terrorising the country's byways and chasing Strava segments – or sipping macchiato and talking about marginal gains.

You've joined the ranks of the MAMILs.

This book is for you. Stay safe out there.

*Local Bike Shop

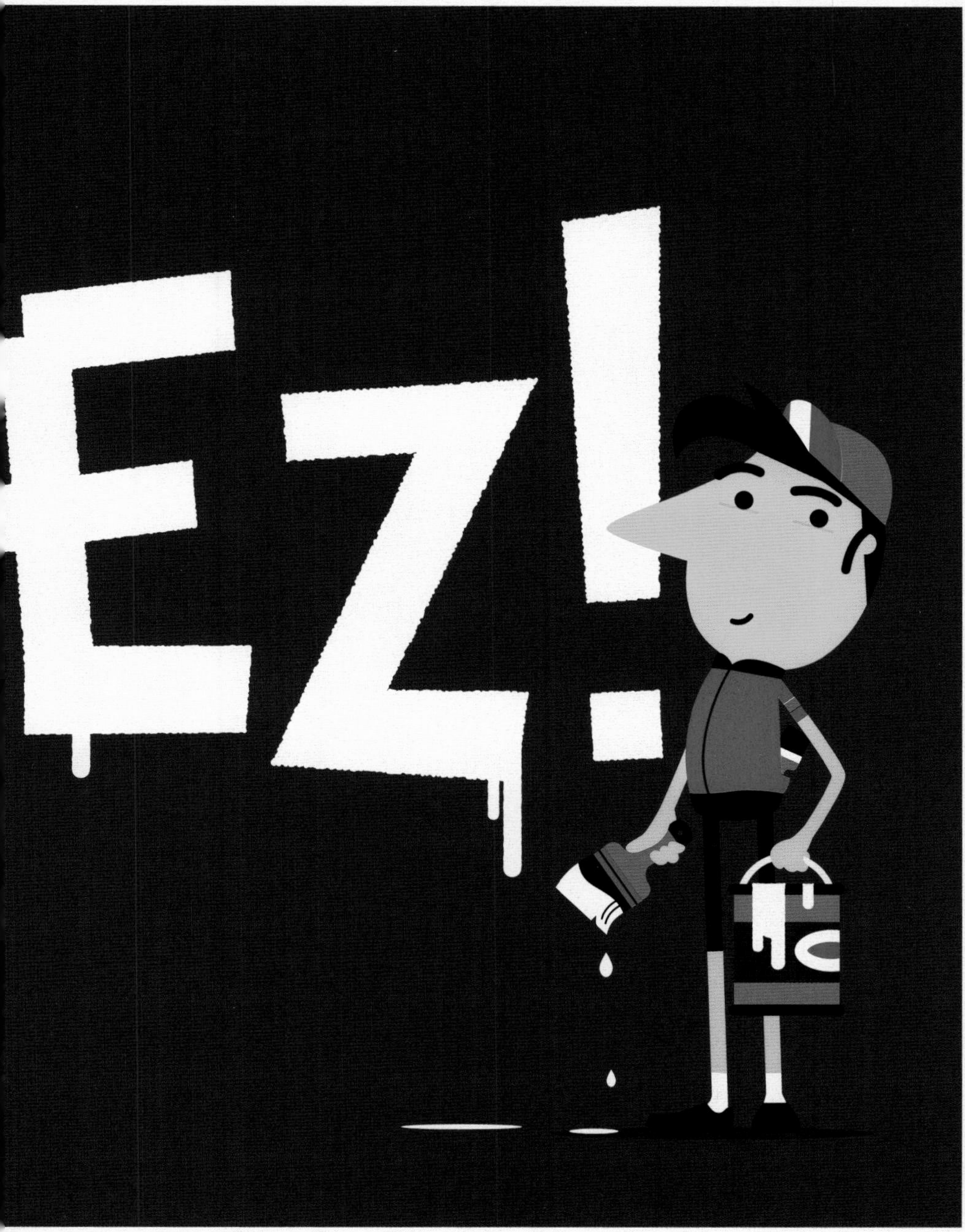
EZ!

ADDICTION

It starts with a little Sunday ride with friends. Soon you're looking for any chance to sneak away, craving those full-day sportives. Your bank balance plummets, the weight falls off you, and your loved ones grow increasingly concerned...

AERO

Not the 1980s chocolate bar. For MAMILs, aero equals SPEED – and you need to feast on it. Hours are spent online in search of the fastest wheels, the most streamlined helmet, the best tuck position and possibly... just maybe... the justification to shave your legs.

ALL ABOUT THE BIKE

MAMILs aspire towards obsessiveness, even devotion. Pro cyclist Sean Kelly was interviewed after the 1984 Amstel Gold Race. He spotted his wife leaning against his car and interrupted the interview to tell her to get off the paintwork. She shrugged. "In your life the car comes first, then the bike, then me." His retort? "You got the order wrong. The bike comes first."

ANAEROBIC

When you're cycling so fast your muscles run out of oxygen.

ANKLING

A seated pedal technique to aid high climbing – ignored by most MAMILs who gear up out of the saddle.

AUDAX

Long-distance cycling with a Gallic flavour, where mudguards are de rigeur. Favoured by the 60+, it's what you do when your sportive budget is spent.

AVERAGE SPEED

The MAMIL's quest for increased speed will know no bounds. A lighter bike, aero wheels, carbon everything and shaved legs will all help reduce the average speed over a club or solo ride.

A

Attack!

The moment when you push hard on the pedals to gain a leading margin. Ideally you will take your competitors unawares – even if those competitors are purely in your imagination.

B

Bonk

You've run out of energy bars and the tank is empty... each turn of the pedals feels like wading through treacle, and you can't tell which side of the road you're on. Yes, you've 'bonked'. Your options are A) Man up and crawl back at a snails' pace or B) Concede defeat, swallow your pride and phone home. What would Wiggins do?

SHUDA ETON

BANANAS

Is that a banana in your, pocket? Actually it's two. The cyclist's best friend, in biodegradable wrapping, this snack is the perfect way to refuel on your Gran Fondo.

BASE MILES

Whilst the 'softer' riders hunker down at home, you are out laying down some long, steady base miles ready for the season ahead. You'll blow them away. If you haven't caught pneumonia first.

BELGIAN BOOTIES

A type of external sock, to keep your carbon shoes gleaming like new. Worse than useless in any weather except sunshine.

BIB SHORTS

When you first dipped your toe into middle-aged cycling, you couldn't believe that anyone would wear bib shorts – the mid-century bather look. Then came the chafing and the chills. Now your wardrobe boasts a handsome selection of these cheese-paring beauties. Just don't wear them as underwear to the office.

BIDONS

What your partner mistakenly calls your water bottle.

BIG-RING RIDERS

Old-school MAMILs who like to slowly grind away in the biggest gear.

BUNNY-HOP

Skillfully avoid that pothole with a cheeky bunny-hop, turning the clock back to when you were 12 on your BMX. But make sure you clear it or you face a 20-minute tube change and some angry fellow riders.

BRAKE RUB

If you're finding the ride even harder than usual, could your brakes be rubbing on your rims? The perennial concern for the ever-paranoid MAMIL (see X for eXcuses).

BREAKAWAY

Your chance at some race glory. You're feeling good and decide to split from the peleton for a breakaway. But always remember that the chasing pack can outpace any lone attacker over distance. Time your move wisely.

CADENCE

Measure of your pedal-turning speed. RPM to the uninitiated. Chris Froome revs at over 100. Olympic triathlon champions the Brownlee brothers recommend a training cadence of 80–90. What's your elusive sweet spot?

CARB-LOADING

A large pizza for a starter? Don't mind if I do.

CAV

Mark Cavendish. The Manx Missile. Simply the greatest sprinter ever. So great that the Tour de France changed its rules to enable him to win a Green Jersey. Allegedly.

CHAIN GANG

A group ride with no stops. Ride hard or get left behind.

CHAPEAU

Literally meaning 'hat' in French, drop this phrase to give respect to other riders.

CHAIN-RING TATTOO

Oily pattern on your inner calf. The mark of a novice.

CHAMOIS

Pronounced 'shammy' This is the only protection between you and your stiff carbon seat... Inspect carfeully when buying shorts.

CHAMOIS CREAM

Man's best thing. Apply liberally before your next sportive to avoid chafing.

CHICKED

When a MAMIL is easily overtaken by a female rider (a Middle-Aged Maiden in Lycra).

C

Carbon

Lightweight, stiff and expensive, this wonder material is the first choice of any self-respecting MAMIL. Carbon frame, carbon pedals, carbon pants…Thousands of pounds will be thrown away in the effort to shave a couple of grams from your bike.

CLIMBERS
MAMILs who weigh under 65kg or own a lot of carbon may fall into the 'Climber' category – see S for Style. With an excellent-power-to weight ratio they're able to race up the hills, usually talking to the rider next to them.

CLIPPED IN
It's a rite of passage for the aspiring MAMIL: pulling up confidently at a roundabout, followed by a slow sideways fall. Yup, you forgot to unclip your bike shoes from your pedals. Again.

COFFEE STOPS
You've ridden 50 miles in the driving wind and rain. You deserve that double espresso and large slab of double chocolate cake. Eat up.

CRITERIUM (CRIT)
A multi-lap race over a short course. Fast and fun. You speed round inches from your fellow riders, so hold your line and leave a little in your tank for a sprint crash… or rather a sprint finish.

CYCLOCROSS
Cycling on dirt trails (without the fear factor of pure mountain biking).

DANCING

On the pedals – like El Pistolero Alberto Contador.

DEEP SECTIONS

Expensive aero carbon rims.

DESCENTS

Strange as it might seem, in a competitive race your descending skills can be as important as your fitness levels. It all comes down to knowing when to apply the brakes – and sheer nerves. Know your limits and watch for bumps, or things will get messy.

DIDI THE DEVIL

The famous costumed figure of the Tour crowd, he capers around and nearly knocks the leaders off their bikes.

DIRECTEUR SPORTIF

On the grand tours, each team's *directeur sportif* sits in the lead car following his key riders and barks instructions down the radio mic. MAMILs can channel their inner *directeur* as a form of self-motivation.

DRAFTING

A fine art – and the difference between amateurs and serious MAMILs. Drafting is quite simply following the wheel of another rider – so closely that they shelter you from the wind and even pull you along in their air pocket. Done right it can save you up to 40% of your energy expenditure (remember that if you stop pedalling, you stop – unless you're connected by a rope). Drafting at speed is fraught with risk, but the rewards are high. Always be aware of when it's your turn to go to the front.

DROPPED

One minute you're happily cycling along in a pack, enjoying the camaraderie and the views. The next minute you're struggling for air as the peleton surges on. As you watch the back end of the back rider disappear over the horizon, you know you've been dropped.

DOMESTIQUES

Grafter who keeps you fuelled throughout the race. Like an obedient puppy. 'Fetch, boy.'

D

Domestique

ELASTIC

The invisible connection between you and the peleton... Stretch it too far and '– snap –' you're off the back . Make sure you hydrate and eat regularly to aviod a solo ride home.

ENDO

Overenthusiastic use of front brake.

ENERGY GELS

Fill up your jersey pockets with this rocket fuel, preferably with added caffeine. Over time you'll become a connoisseur of brands and flavours ('I prefer the 2012 GU Vanilla Bean – it has grassy overtones and a clean finish…').

EPIC

This climb is epic, this view is epic, this epic is epic.

EPO

MAMILs can tut-tut all they like about pro cheats, but if EPO transfusions were legalised they'd be first in the queue.

ERECTILE DYSFUNCTION

There's no link between this and excessive hours on the bike. Definitely not. Just don't Google it.

ESSENTIALS

The kit you'll need for each ride. Spare tube, cash, credit card, phone, zip ties, multitool, gilet (or spare top), mini pump, tyre patches, chain links, gels/bars, water. This needs to fit into a couple of tiny pockets (or get a *domestique*).

ETAPES

A pilgrimage to the home of cycling. You'll ride a stage of the Tour de France with a thousand or so other riders. Just don't get off and walk – then you'll be collected by cart.

EYEWEAR

You'll need three pairs: clear, tinted, polarised. They must be streamlined, vented and most importantly clip into the top of your aero helmet when climbing (and round the back for coffee breaks).

E

Espresso

The only acceptable way to take your mid-ride caffeine fix (also see M for Machiatto). A true MAMIL will also invest in a high-end espresso maker, even if it leaves no kitchen room for a microwave oven or kettle.

Velopress
COFFEE CO.

COF

Espresso
Macchia
American
Latte
Cappuccin

FAMILY
The impediment to your training regime.

FEED ZONES
To be found on sportives, this is the place to stock up on gels and energy bars for future rides.

FIZZ
Energy to the layman. Use it wisely. Each time you spend some 'fizz' you get closer to the red zone.

FLAMME ROUGE
Not a shot of something horrible you slam at the end of a night out, but the red kite that marks the last kilometre of a bike race.

FLEMISH FACIALS
The fine coating of mud, dust and grit that indicates an epic ride in testing conditions. Named after the classic Belgian cobbled races.

FOOD LOG
Crucial to calculate your calorie offsetting, e.g. a two-hour ride justifies the consumption of four Peronis and a large calzone.

FORM
That elusive thing.

FOXING
Not showing all your cards. Saving yourself.

FRANCE
The spiritual home of the MAMIL, *bien sûr*.

FULL GAS
Going from standing to pushing as hard as you can, leaving everything you have on the road...use with a Dutch inflection for extra emphasis. 'Full gasss!'

FULL-KIT W*NKER (FKW)
The MAMIL faux pas. Never wear full kit that matches your bike – otherwise known as Mr BMC – it will quickly mark you out as a FKW.

F

Full tuck

Hugging the topbar, elbows and knees
tucked in. This kamikaze aero position
should only be adopted once you've spun
out on a descent (if you need some lessons,
check out the master Peter Sagan).

GARMIN
Tech of choice for the discerning rider. Upgrade regularly and bemoan when it takes you off route.

GC
General Classification. The best overall competing rider of the Tour victory – for example, the Yellow Jersey in the Tour de France.

GCN (Global Cycling Network)
Makers of addictive YouTube videos – ideal viewing on those productive Friday afternoons in the office.

GLUTES
Men store fat in their butts, so tight glutes are a sign of form. Pros have been known to give rivals a squeeze.

GRAN FONDO
A long-distance race, where riders are chip-timed and have the right of way at all intersections. The tradition began in Italy in the 70s as a way to sort the pros from the wannabes. Try your own – if you can handle 200km of riding and 3,000 metres of climbs.

GRANNY GEAR
The lowest gear on your bike. When going up the gradients 'What's not in your legs needs to be in your gears'.

Goldi Socks

Not too high, not too low. Sock length and colour can quickly mark you as a novice so get it right - white (exception for black may be made if it matches your kit), and 6 inches above the shoe.

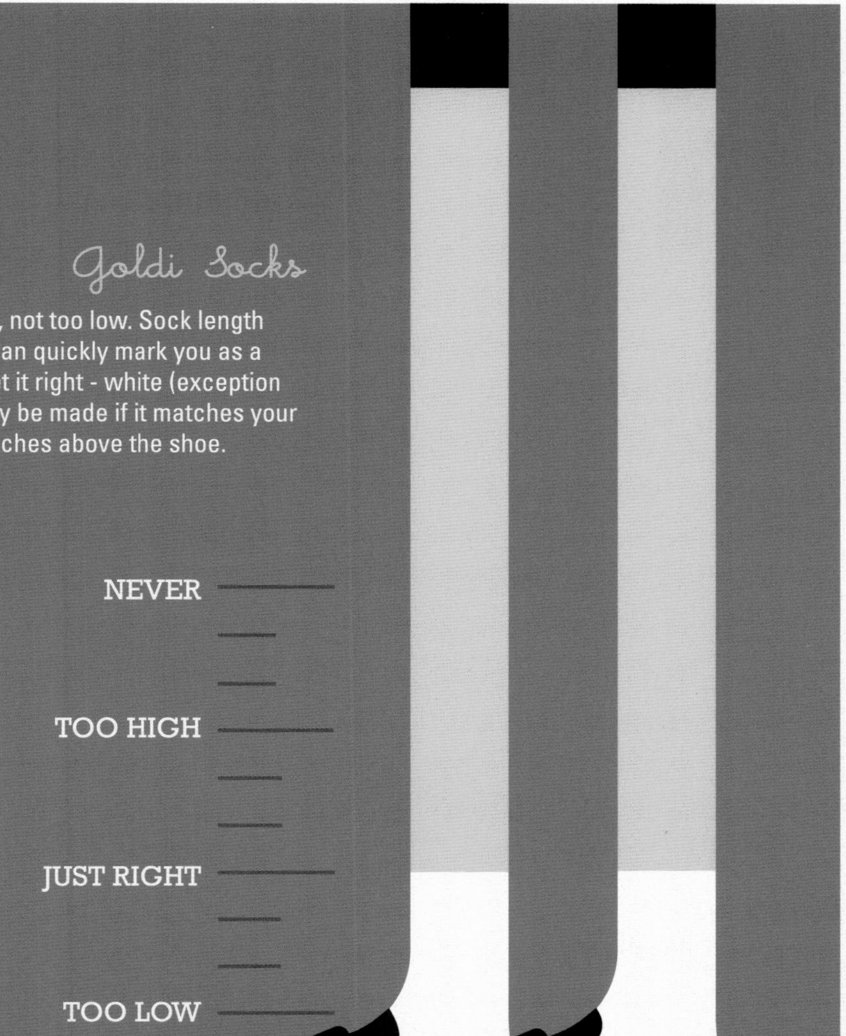

NEVER

TOO HIGH

JUST RIGHT

TOO LOW

HALF-WHEELING
Nudging ahead of the rider next to you until your speed increases to 'Full gasss!'

HAMMER
It's time to go large and stick it in the big gear, crank out some serious wattage until the elastic snaps. Or you hit a slight incline.

HAND SIGNALS
The lead rider's responsibility. Point at potholes. Wiggle fingers for gravel. Wave for cars. Hand up for stop and an awkward arm reach around for overtaking.

HANGING IN
You've raised your game and decided to ride with the fast group, but the pace is relentless and your heart rate is in the red. Gasping for oxygen and necking some gels you're almost off the back and hanging in for the coffee stop.
There is a coffe stop, right...?

HEART-RATE MONITORS
Sitting on your handlebars like a devil on your shoulder, your bike computer relays your heart rate and never lets you rest. Slavishly you strain to stay in your zones. It must be obeyed.

HOLD YOUR LINE!
You're travelling tightly bunched into a corner. Lightly feather the brakes, keep it loose on the bars and feel like you're part of a pro peleton by telling your fellow riders to "hold your line!" – remember inside is suicide.

HOODS
A relaxed position for taking selfies whilst riding.

HTFU
Harden the Fuck Up. No moaning in the wet and cold.

Hills...

...are pills, prescribed by the doctor of pain. Find some categorised climbs and take as often as you can. Welcome to the 'Hurt Zone'.

Italian

When ordering cycle gear online, always remember that a large size Italian will only fit a very small boy in English. Size up if you want to be able to breathe.

INCLINES
"Are we going uphill? This must be an incline – what's the gradient?"

IN THE RED
Each time you push hard on those pedals and 'burn matches' you go into the red. But be careful: you only have a certain number left in the box (see D for Dropped).

INTERNET
A handy computer-based network used to share tips with fellow MAMILS, and to purchase essential kit.

INTERVALS
Intense bursts of 30 seconds to one minute. If practised on a turbo trainer, intervals are powerful tools to increase fitness and race performance. You tell yourself that you'll do more of them, but you never do.

JENS VOIGT

Jens. Jensie. The German. Suave, record-breaking Criterium legend, known for his aggressive attacks and for the moment he borrowed a child's bike to complete 15km of the Tour de France. His signature phrase 'Shut Up, Legs!' has been adopted as the official MAMIL anthem.

JERSEYS

Must be as tight as possible – flapping material is an aero enemy. If you insist on wearing the colours of a pro team, don't try to match it with shorts or socks. Ideally you should acquire vintage or keep new jerseys for a few years before use – thus looking like you've always been a fan of the team.

JOIN A CLUB

The roads can be a lonely place on your own... plus a riding sat in a group uses 40% less energy. Join a club and see those Strava average speeds rise.

Juice

Forget EPO, testosterone and the underground IV hook-ups that plagued the peleton in the past and get 'juiced' the natural way. Beetroot has been proven to aid the uptake of oxygen to blood, so inject a shot an hour before a ride, just don't tell your fellow riders.

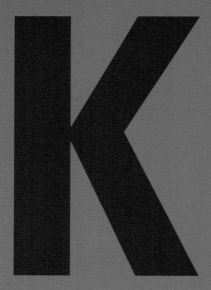

KILOMETRES
Distances and speeds are always measured in km. Miles are for runners.

KOM
King of the Mountains. The title awarded to the best climber; a race within a race.

KUDOS
Cyclist unit of praise, made ubiquitous by Strava. The online equivalent of '*chapeau*'.

LANCE
He who shall not be named. The touchstone for all that is wrong in modern cycling.

LANTERNE ROUGE
Competitor who finishes last, or the MAMIL who buys the first round.

LBS (LOCAL BIKE SHOPS)
Meeting place for the like-minded. Get to know yours well. From servicing your gears to chatting about which lube to use over an espresso – try sourcing that on a German internet bike retailer. But exercise caution: you'll wander in looking for a new pump, and emerge with a £1,500 groupset.

LEAN
An aspirational state.

LIDS
The MAMIL's term for a helmet, just make sure it's black or white and well ventilated as you don't want to look like a multicoloured sweaty clown.

LUBE
Wet, dry. No, this is not the shopping list for a brothel. It's FOR YOUR CHAIN.

LUMPY
A hilly ride.

LSD (Long Slow Distance)

Favoured by earlier generations of MAMILs, the ethos of LSD is all about epic day-long rides. Some old-school coaches still argue that LSD is the only way to get enough 'miles in your legs'. That means more than 500 miles a week – whatever the weather.

10

Cycling Legends

The Cannibal, EDDY MERCKX
The Lion King, MARIO CIPOLLINI
Monsieur Chrono, JACQUES ANQUETIL
~~*Big Tex*, LANCE ARMSTRONG~~
The Badger, BERNARD HINAULT.
Big Mig, MIGUEL INDURAIN
L'Americain, GREG LEMOND
King Kelly, SEAN KELLY
The Professor, LAURENT FIGNON
The Jensie, JENS VOIGT

Il Campionissimo, Fausto Coppi

MACCHIATO
An espresso with some foamed milk. Must be consumed whilst checking Strava.

MAILLOT JAUNE
Much copied, never bettered. Since 1919, the leader of the General Classification in the Tour de France wears the *Maillot Jaune* – the Yellow Jersey.

MALLORCA
Idyllic Spanish retreat where pro teams, including Team Sky, spend their winter seasons. The local government has helpfully responded by tarmacking new bike lines across the island. This has encouraged MAMILs to holiday there en masse, spending their mornings desperately trying to hold the pace of Richie Porte and Geraint Thomas, and their afternoons sipping *cerveza*. Bliss.

MALT LOAVES
The strapped-for-cash cyclists' fuel. Yours for 99p a mega-loaf.

MARGINAL GAINS
Creed of continual, incremental improvement to every aspect of your preparation and performance. Made famous – and devastatingly effective – by Sir Dave Brailsford at British Cycling and then Team Sky. Adopted by MAMILs as an excuse to focus on minor details (e.g. the weight of the eyewear) rather than the big picture (e.g. the 'marginal gains' from a lamb bhuna every Friday night).

MECHANICAL
The weather's closing in and you're halfway home, putting the power down ascending a local climb when – 'clunk' – your derailleur decides to make a crunching noise, or worse still your chain breaks. Time to do some maintenance, or invest in electronic gears.

MUSETTES
The only acceptable man bag, usually used for food.

Snap, crackle, pop... clunk!

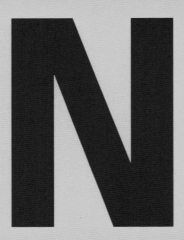

N

(N)+1
The formula indicating the number of bikes that a MAMIL needs. Where (N) equals current number of bikes owned.

NATURAL BREAKS
A loo stop. But if you're in the peleton, just hold it in.

NIRVANA
To the uninitiated, Holland must sound like a cyclist's paradise – some 40% of all journeys in Amsterdam are made by bike. But MAMILs don't dream of gently pedalling alongside a canal. Oh no. Their personal Nirvana is probably the summit of Mont Ventoux on the Tour – bleak, bare, boiling hot and the place where cycling legends are made.

NO PANTS
Shorts are designed to be worn commando style – with no pants – so make sure your Lycra is expensive and non-see-through.

NUTRITION
Don't kid yourself.

OMERTÀ
The secret cycle code. What goes on in the peleton...stays in the peleton.

OLD-TIMERS
Hard-as-nails older rider, usually sports a big beard, wears a cap in favour of a helmet and a woollen jersey over the modern Lycra worn by MAMILs. The old-timer is capable of grinding out a tempo on little more than water so make sure you respect your elders.

ON THE RIVET
Sitting right on the edge of your seat, putting the power down. The phrase comes from the old leather saddles.

ONE-HOUR RECORD
Long forgotten, the one-hour record sprang back into vogue in 2014 when the UCI modified the rules to level the playing field. It's brutally simple: how far can you ride in an hour? If you are Sir Bradley Wiggins, the answer is a record-breaking 54.526km.

OVERSHOES
Neoprene or waterproof shoe covers. Unlike a Belgian bootie these are a must.

OWN THE ROAD
Never ride 2 inches from the gutter. It's strewn with rubbish, potholes and encourages cars to overtake when they shouldn't. Safer to ride at least a metre from the kerb, and when approaching traffic-calming measures to move to the middle and 'own the road'.

PAIN CAVE

The place you go for a gruelling physical workout. "If I want to get faster on the bike, I've gotta do my workout, so I am headed to the pain cave." See S for Sufferfest.

PALAEO DIET

'I'm going Palaeo this season.' Involves only eating foods that were consumed by hominids in the Paleolithic Age, which ended around 10,000 BC. No wheat, no sugar, no alcohol. As with most diet plans made by MAMILs, your resolution will last until the first long ride of the season. After more than four hours in the saddle you'll be speed-dialling Domino's. That's fine – you definitely need to 'bulk up' anyway…

PAYPAL

The stealth method to hide your purchases from Wiggle and other well-known online retailers.

PEANUT BUTTER

Possibly the most energy-packed of all spreads. Acceptable to scoop direct from the jar after a heavy ride.

PELETON

A large formation of riders.

POWER-TO-WEIGHT RATIO

Beloved topic of all hill climbers. Lose the flab or build your quads. The choice is yours.

PREPARATION

Fail to prepare… prepare to fail.

PRETZELS

A badly buckled wheel.

PSI

Pounds per square inch – this can be found on your tyres. Debated endlessly: front, rear, wet and dry.

P

Pothole

HOLE!!! Up goes the call from the rider inches in front.
Too late to swerve and no time to bunny-hop, your
thousand-pound carbon rims take a smash and down you go.
If you're lucky it's a simple flat, not an insurance claim.

QOM
Queen of the Mountain, but can you beat her time?

QUADDAGE
The shape and output of your quadriceps are now up for public scrutiny. Everyone can have a squeeze.

QUIET
No creaks, no squeaks, no crunching gears or annoying clicking noises... the only sound you should hear on your ride is the heavy breathing from your fellow riders as you put the hammer down. Grease up.

You've been 'chicked'

Quotes

Memorise some classic quotes — and draw on them as inspiration to summit that next climb.

"Don't buy upgrades, ride up grades."

~ Eddy Merckx

"It never gets easier – you just go faster."

~ Greg LeMond

"As long as I breathe, I attack."

~ Bernard Hinault

"Crashing is part of cycling as crying is part of love."

~ Johan Museeuw

"Training is like fighting a gorilla. You don't stop when you're tired; you stop when the gorilla's tired."

~ Greg Henderson

RAPHA

The brand that puts the 'L' in MAMIL. This young British company makes aspirational kit, with each hand-crafted sensual piece costing more than a Dolce & Gabbana dress and holding the promise of transforming your performance and lifestyle. 'Rapha is more than just a product company… it is an online emporium of performance roadwear, accessories, publications and events, all celebrating the glory and suffering of road riding.' Ahem.

RECOVERY ALES

Craft beer is now almost as crucial to MAMIL culture as espresso. A couple of pints of local-brewed pale ale are applauded as part of your recovery regime – what better way to pack in carbs, protein *and* sugar?

RED ZONE

Cycling at a heart rate that can only be sustained for a few seconds before you 'blow up'.

RELAX

If you hate the descents, then it's time you relaxed. Use a soft grip on the handlebars, loosen your shoulders and… chill.

ROAD RASH

Allergic reaction between skin and tarmac accentuated by friction. Treated with iodine and tweezers.

ROLLERS

Pop your bike on a set of rollers and not even a snowstorm will stop you turning the wheels. Best kept in the garage or shed – otherwise known as the pain cave – unless you are single or very confident about the strength of your relationship.

ROULEURS

A rider who pushes a steady big gear over a long distance on the flat.

SCR

Silly commuter racing. Your attempt to retake the record on the 200-metre Post Office-to-Asda sprint becomes the highlight of your working day.

SHAVING

In the pursuit of marginal gains and saving a few valuable minutes you'll be prepared to shave most of your body... and you may even like it.

SHUT UP, LEGS

See J for Jens Voigt.

SLAMMED

Ride like the pros, remove all spacers and slam the stem. You'll need to be flexible. See Y for Yoga.

SPEED

A life long investment of time and money.

SPINNING

Turning your pedals like billy-o to get up a hill. "Spinners are winners."

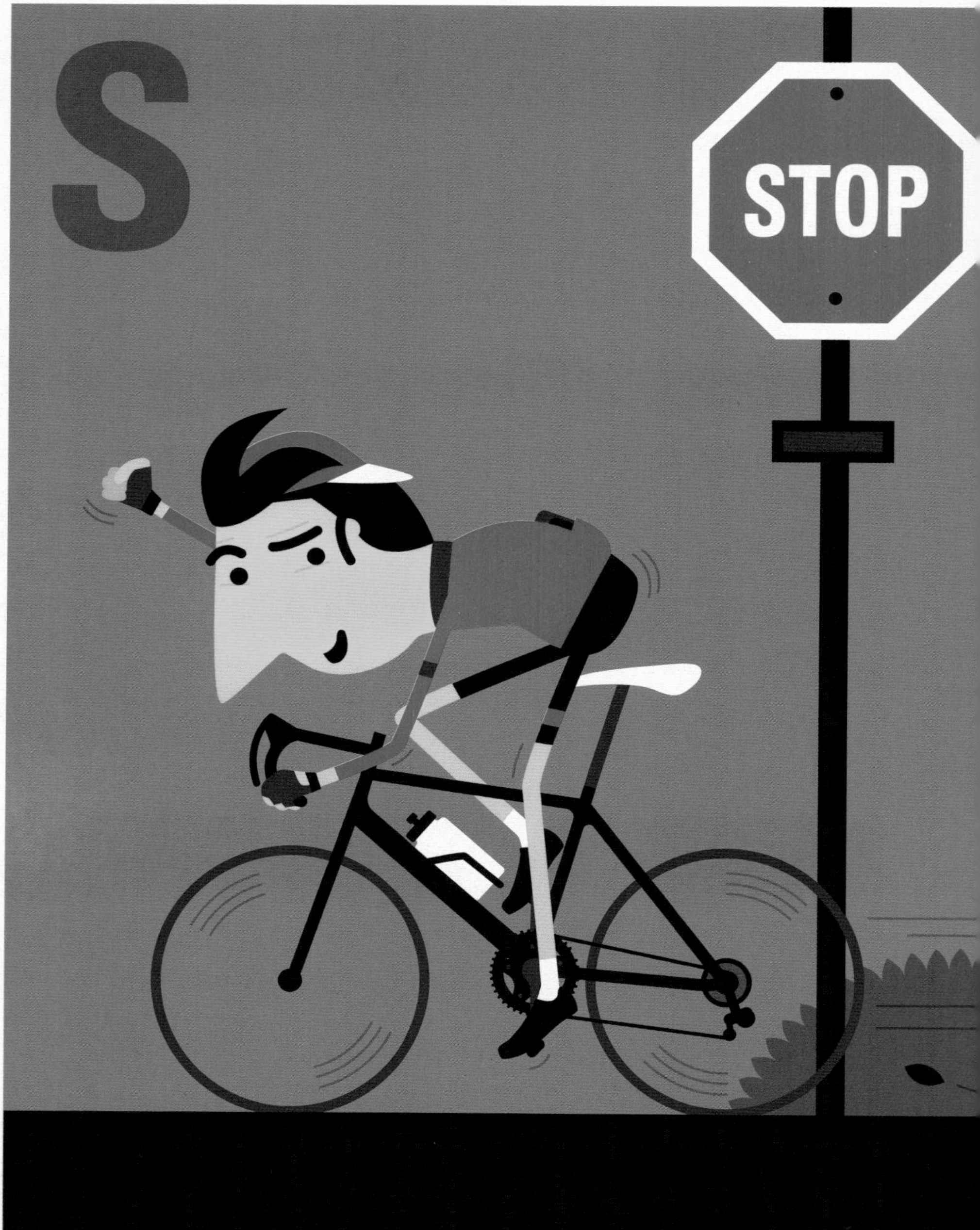
S
STOP

SPORTIVE
A large meeting of like-minded MAMILs wishing to ride 100km of countryside.

SPRINTERS
MAMILs who shelter in packs whilst on the club run, only to pop up and race anyone to a sign or coffee shop.

SPRINTING FOR SIGNS
Your urban version of an Olympic time trial. Last to the STOP sign gets the espressos in.

STIFF
Worrying term of endearment for all bike parts ('My new crank is so stiff').

STRAVA
Every MAMIL's favourite app. Log all your rides and get super competitive with Bryan in Australia as you rack up the miles and increase your average speed. Break down every aspect of your ride, and see if you broke a record on any segments. Just watch you don't spend more time on Strava than actually cycling.

STYLE (RIDING)
What style of rider are you? Climber, Sprinter, Rouleur, Time Triallist.

SUFFERFEST
What you experience on the way to the Suffersphere. See V for the velominati.

SUMMER BIKES
Your best bike, no mudguards, no messing, never gets wet.

TAN LINES

These lines (dividing pasty white from deep bronze skin) are a clear sign of heroic hours on the bike.

TECHNOLOGY

Otherwise referred to as toys, a MAMIL is never without the latest tech, power meters, electric gears, heartrate monitors, cadence sensors…

TEMPO

Riding pace just above slow and below 'I can't talk right now'.

THRESHOLD

Cycling at your max before your heart and lungs explode. Your FTP (Functional Threshold Power) is around 90% of your peak power.

TIME TRIALS

The clue is in the title. Cycle as hard and fast as you can for a specified time without throwing up. At least until the time's up. Time Triallists like to identify themselves by wearing even tighter Lycra – skinsuits – and sperm-shaped aero helmets whilst adopting a spine-crunching superman riding position.

TITANIUM

Some MAMILs swear by it.

TRACK STANDS

Approaching a set of lights or junction, you may decide to test your track stand. That's holding your bike upright with the minimum of movement. Impressive… Just make sure you're ready to unclip.

TUBS

Tubular tyres that don't require an inner tube. Used by the pros and racers alike. If you want fast and light, then tubular are the way to go. But if you do puncture roadside be prepared for a messy fix.

TURN ON THE FRONT

Don't be a 'wheel-sucker' or hide at the back annoying your fellow riders and letting them do all the work. Make sure you take your rolling turn unless you've hit the wall.

T

Best in Club

UCI

Cycling's global governing body, somewhat tarnished by its complicity with Lance and the doping era. Can be used as a pejorative phrase for any ineffectual rules or bureaucracy.

UNDER THE COSH

A feeling of relentless pressure, keeping you outside your comfort zone. Usually experienced when you've latched on to a group who are a few notches above you.

UPGRADES

True, Eddie Merckx once said "You don't buy upgrades, you ride up grades", but in the world of the MAMIL this can be discounted. It's fine to obsess about the latest wearable tech, deep-section carbon rims, power meter or even the most fashionable shade of Lycra. Fine.

If Eddie had Mastercard

V

Welcome to the Suffersphere

VELOCIPEDES

A human-powered land vehicle with one or more wheels.

VELOMINATI

The Velominati are like a two-wheeled fight club. These self-styled 'Keepers of the Cog' have drawn up a gloriously dictatorial set of rules for MAMILs to live by. Some of our favourites:

Rule #7 //   Tan lines should be cultivated and kept razor sharp.

Rule #34 //   Mountain bike shoes and pedals have their place. On a mountain bike.

Rule #55 //   Earn your turns. If you are riding down a mountain, you must first have ridden up the mountain. It is forbidden to employ powered transportation simply for the cheap thrill of descending.

Rule #71 //   Train Properly. Know how to train properly and stick to your training plan. Ignore other cyclists with whom you are not intentionally riding. The time for being competitive is not during your training rides, but during competition.

See www.velominati.com for more of this sado-masochistic MAMIL code.

VELOPORN

Spending too long looking at hi-res pictures of top-range new bikes. You'll go blind.

VETERANS

You in any competitive event post 40.

VO² MAX

For sports scientists and cycle geeks. This is a measure of the maximum volume of oxygen that an athlete can use, millilitres per kilogram of body weight per minute (ml/kg/min). Essentially it shows how quickly you hit the red zone.

WALL
You've hit it again.

WATTAGE
Another stat to obsess over.

WEIGHT
'How much does yours [bike] weigh?'
'How much does that new seat weigh?'
'How much does air weigh?'

WHEEL-SUCKERS
A rider who drafts behind the group for most of the sportive, conserving energy, then challenges you to race with half a kilometre to go.

WHEELS
Like eyewear, you'll need three sets. Wheels for everyday training, deep-section carbon aero wheels for speed and a set of lightweight rims for climbing... and maybe one more set for racing.

WIGGO (BRADLEY)
Modfather of cycling and first British winner of the Tour de France.

WINTER
Your love for riding has no limits. Not even driving rain with a −3°C wind chill.

WINTER BIKES
The one with mudguards. Justifies the purchase of a new Summer Bike.

Take your turn

X,Y&Z

eXCUSES

The MAMIL is master of the excuse.
The wrong hill: 'I'm really more of a sprinter'.
The wrong flat run: 'I'm really more of a climber'.
The wrong bike: 'If I'd known we were doing climbs I'd have brought my aero bike'.
The wrong day: 'This is really more of a recovery ride for me – I went hard yesterday'.

eXHAUSTION

You'll be tired after a morning's ride so settle into a comfy chair, switch on Eurosport and catch up with the latest Grand Tour.

YOGA

Every MAMIL should practise yoga. Nobody does, until they get injured.

ZIP TIES

The utility fastener for any roadside emergency.

ZONES

When cycling with serious intent, you're usually aiming to get 'in the zone'. This is an unspecified place where your legs turn of their own accord, your focus is absolute, and you achieve a zen-like oneness with your bike. It lasts for mere seconds and is instantly broken by potholes, traffic lights or silly comments from fellow riders.

Spencer Wilson

is an illustrator and designer of
sorts. After a glorious football
career he now has both feet
firmly clicked into the MAMIL
camp. He lives in the cyclists'
nirvana of Hertfordshire with his
support crew – his wife Anna
and daughters Gracie and Isla.
He rides as much as he can
with Berkhamsted and Hemel
Hempstead cycle clubs... and
spends far too much time
looking at Veloporn.

By the same authors:

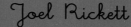

Joel Rickett

is a publisher, author and wannabe MAMIL. He lives in north London with his wife Siân and girls Sophie and Esme (budding Queens of the Mountains). He is the proud owner of an entry-level road bike which is tragically underused – although he does appreciate the difference between a macchiato and a cortado. His riding style is very much like his dancing style, which was once compared to 'Bambi on acid'.

ACKNOWLEDGEMENTS

It takes a peleton to produce a book like this, backed up by a support team to rival Team Sky's back office.

Thank you to all the MAMILs who helped us put this crazy world into words. True to the book we'll list them in alphabetical order: Dan Barton, Nick (Velo) Clark, Neill Furmston, Trevor Hill, Matt Long, Tori Madine, Mike McMahon and Stuart Ratcliffe
Thank you to our publisher Etta Saunders, at the small but beautifully formed Kinkajou imprint of Frances Lincoln. The best ideas can come from the nicest lunches (aided by a few Recovery Ales).

Thank you to our unstoppable, unbelievably good licensing agents Sue Bateman and Jehane Boden Spiers at Yellow House in Brighton.

You can find The Modern MAMIL on www.facebook.com/modernmamil

Also in this series:

* Middle Aged Man In Lycra

the
MODERN MAMIL*
A CYCLIST'S JOURNAL
Spencer Wilson & Joel Rickett